Contents

Words in **bold** are in the glossary on page 23.

Blue planet

We all live on Planet Earth. Earth is made of rock and is round, like a ball.

Blue ocean covers most of Earth's **surface**. Land covers the rest.

Clouds float in the air above the oceans and the land.

We live on Earth. It has land and sea.

Frozen zones

The Arctic and Antarctica are the coldest places on Earth.

The Arctic is found in the far north of the planet and Antarctica is in the far south.

Antarctica is covered by ice all year round.

Polar bears live in the frozen Arctic. They have lots of fat and thick fur to keep them warm.

The Arctic and Antarctic are very cold. Polar bears live in the Arctic. Their thick fur keeps them warm.

Dry deserts

Deserts are the most dry and **barren** places on Earth.

The ground is covered with sand or stones.

It hardly ever rains in a desert, but desert animals are well **adapted** to live without much water. Camels can survive for ten days without drinking.

Deserts are dry.
Camels can live
in the desert.
They do not have
to drink very often.

9

Rainforests

A rainforest gets lots of rain. Many different animals and plants are found here.

It rains hard every day in a **tropical** rainforest.

Plants grow close together, and trees can grow to be very tall.

Insects buzz in the air, snakes slither along the ground and monkeys and birds chatter in the trees.

11

Coral reefs

The oceans are wide and deep and filled with saltwater.

Colourful **coral reefs** grow in warm, **shallow** sea close to land.

Many sea creatures live around coral reefs. They include little clown fish and big reef sharks.

Coral reefs are found in warm sea. Big and little fish live near coral reefs.

Mountains

The tops of mountains reach
high into the sky.

Some reach higher than the clouds!

A volcano is a mountain that can **erupt**.

Boiling hot runny rock called lava and hot **ash** shoot out of the top and pour down the mountainside.

Mountains are high hills.
Mountains called volcanoes
can erupt. Hot rock shoots out of them.

Running rivers

**A river begins as a little stream.
It gets bigger as it flows to the sea.**

A river flows from hills or mountains
down towards the sea. It begins as
a small, trickling stream.

The river gets wider and slower as it flows across flatter land.

The river mouth is where a river joins the sea. Birds visit river mouths to feed on tiny shellfish and worms.

Grasslands

Grasslands are huge grassy **plains**. They are found in many places on Earth.

Giraffes, zebras, lions and other wild animals live on grasslands in Africa.

In North America, grasslands are called prairies.

Farmers grow wheat, corn and other **cereals** on the prairies.

Grasslands are big places that are covered with grass. Giraffes live on grasslands in Africa.

Where we live

Lots of people live on Earth.
Many work in towns and cities.
Cities have homes and offices.

Billions of people live on Earth. Some live in villages and farms in the countryside.

Others live and work close together in towns and cities. Some people work in offices in very tall buildings called skyscrapers.

Quiz

1. What covers most of Earth's surface?

2. What keeps a polar bear warm?

3. What is a volcano?

4. What is a river mouth?

Glossary

adapted having special features that make a plant or animal able to survive in a place

ash dust and flakes that are made when something burns

barren dry and bare with few plants

cereals wheat, corn, oats and barley and other types of grass that are grown for food

coral reefs places where millions of tiny shellfish grow together

erupt when a volcano spits out hot lava and ash

plains flat, grassy land with few trees

shallow not deep

surface the outer layer of something

tropical very hot

Answers to quiz:
1. The ocean.
2. Thick fur and fat.
3. A mountain that can erupt.
4. Where a river meets the sea.

Index

Franklin Watts
Published in Great Britain in 2017 by
The Watts Publishing Group

Copyright ©The Watts Publishing
Group 2015

Series Editor: Julia Bird
Series Advisor: Karina Law
Series Design: Basement68

Dewey number: 550
ISBN 978 1 4451 3807 7

Picture credits: Dan Breckwoldt/Shutterstock: 21. Craig Burrows/Shutterstock: 8.
Cigdem Sean Cooper/Shutterstock: 13. Dchauy/Shutterstock: 16. Volodymyr Goinyk/
Shutterstock: 6. Pablo Hidalgo/Shutterstock: 1, 15. Jorgefelix/Dreamstime: 17. Leni
Kovaleva/Shutterstock: 4. Lluvatar/Dreamstime: 19. Loskutnikov/Shutterstock: 5. Petr
Mlynek/Dreamstime: 14. Photographerlondon/Dreamstime: 18. Howard Sandler/
Shutterstock: 3b, 11. Skypixel/Dreamstime: front cover. Szefei/Shutterstock: 10.
Turtix/Shutterstock: 20. Masa Ushioda/Alamy: 2, 12. Vibe Images/Shutterstock: 3t, 7.
Wolfgang Zwanzger/Shutterstock: 3c, 9.

Printed in China

Franklin Watts
An imprint of
Hachette Children's Group
Part of The Watts Publishing Group
Carmelite House
50 Victoria Embankment
London EC4Y 0DZ

An Hachette UK Company

www.hachette.co.uk
www.franklinwatts.co.uk

MIX
Paper from
responsible sources
FSC® C104740